I CHOOSE
to Be a Helper

1
CHOOSE
SERIES

ELIZABETH
ESTRADA

I CHOOSE
to Be a Helper

ELIZABETH ESTRADA

I get warm, fuzzy feelings
In my body and **mind**,
Especially when I'm
Caring, helpful, and **kind**.

If someone's in need,
I will do what I **can**.
I'm ready and willing
To lend them a **hand**.

There are dozens of ways
That I can help **out**.
So I've chosen a few
I can tell you **about**.

I can help in the house
With everyday **chores**,
Like setting the table
Or sweeping the **floors**.

I can help with the laundry
Or hang up my **clothes**
After I eat breakfast,
I can wash the cereal **bowls**.

I can take out the garbage
Without being **asked**,
Or work with my dad
When he's cutting the **grass**.

I can water the flowers
Or pull up the **weeds**.
I can help with digging
Or planting some **seeds**.

If my brother is crying,
As babies will **do**,
I can help with a hug
And a snuggle or **two**.

If my sister is struggling
With homework from **school**,
I can easily help out.
It'd be totally **cool**.

I can make sure the rabbit
Has plenty to **eat**.
I can take the dog for a walk
Down the **street**.

I'll try to be giving
In every thoughtful **way**.
"You're amazingly helpful,"
My parents will **say**.

And it's not just at home
Where I can **assist**.
There are lots of ideas
Written down on my **list**.

Whenever I'm at school,
I can help out my **teacher**.
If something needs doing,
I'll choose to be a **helper**.

I can bake some cookies
Or even a **cake**.
If it helps bring a smile,
I'll do what it **takes**.

If a neighbor's in need,
I'll be there right **away**.
But only, of course,
If my mom says **okay**.

I can pet-sit their hamster
Or tortoise or **toad**,
Or pick up their mail,
And bring it in by the **load**.

If they're old, or sick,
Or they're hurt by a **fall**,
I can run them an errand,
No problem at **all**.

With a word or a wave,
I will show them I **care**.
As it's helpful to know
That there's somebody **there**.

Helping out others,
Like my family and **friends**
Is a wonderful thing.
But that's not where it **ends**.

Many might need help,
You can **bet**.
Like the millions of people
I've not even **met**.

I can offer my help
To the girls and the **boys**
Who'd appreciate getting
My unwanted **toys**.

I can take my old clothes
To a charity **store**.
And give them to kids
Who can wear them some **more**.

Any books that I've read
And no longer **need**,
I'll donate to the library
For others to **read**.

I can take all the cash
From my lemonade **stand**
And help feed the hungry
In faraway **lands**.

There is simply no end
To the things I can **do**.
I choose to be a helper.
So, how about **you**?